Origami Architecture

AMERICAN HOUSE

KODANSHA INTERNATIONAL
Tokyo and New York

Origami Architecture

AMERICAN HOUSES

Pre-Colonial to Present

Masahiro Chatani

Introduction by David Stewart
Photographs by Akihiko Tokue

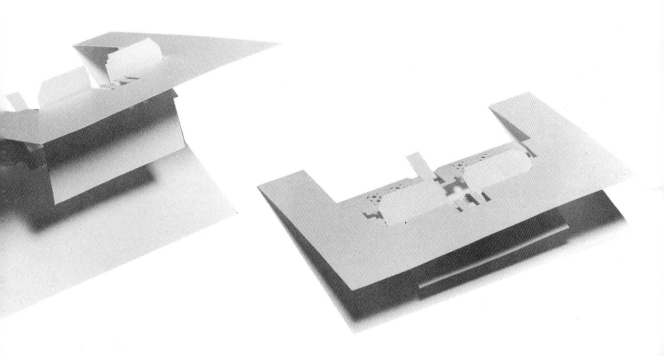

Text on pages 15 to 34 translated by Neil Warren.
Line drawings for same pages by Toshiaki Nakazawa.

The publisher wishes to thank David Stewart and Tokyo Pages
for their assistance in the preparation of this work.

Distributed in the United States by Kodansha International/
USA Ltd., through Harper & Row, Publishers, Inc., 10 East
53rd Street, New York, New York 10022. Published by
Kodansha International Ltd., 2-2, Otowa 1-chome, Bunkyo-
ku, Tokyo 112, and Kodansha International/USA Ltd., 10
East 53rd Street, New York, New York 10022.

ISBN 0-87011-837-4 (U.S.)
ISBN 4-7700-1337-X (Japan)

Library of Congress Cataloging-in-Publication Data
Chatani, Masahiro, 1934–
    Origami architecture.

    Bibliography: p.
    1. Paper work.   2. Architecture, Domestic—
United States. I. Title.
TT870.C46 1988   736'.982   87-82864

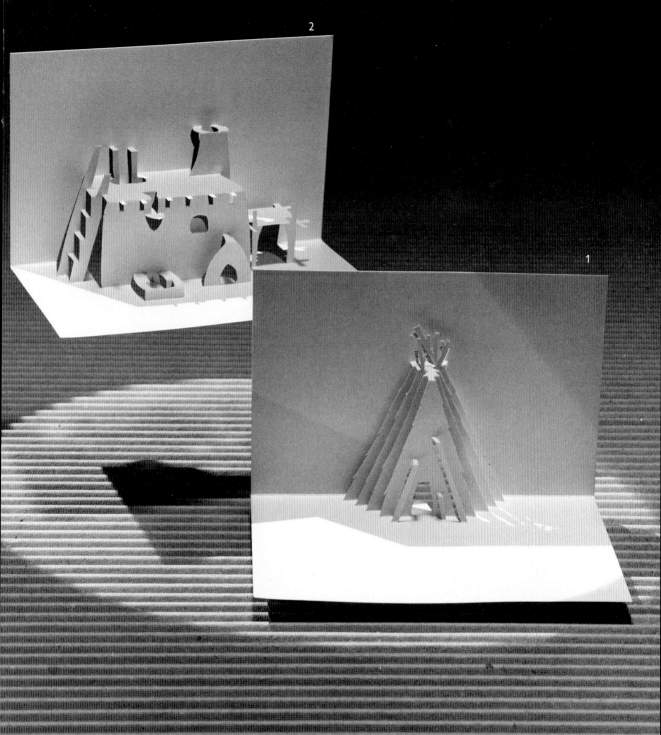

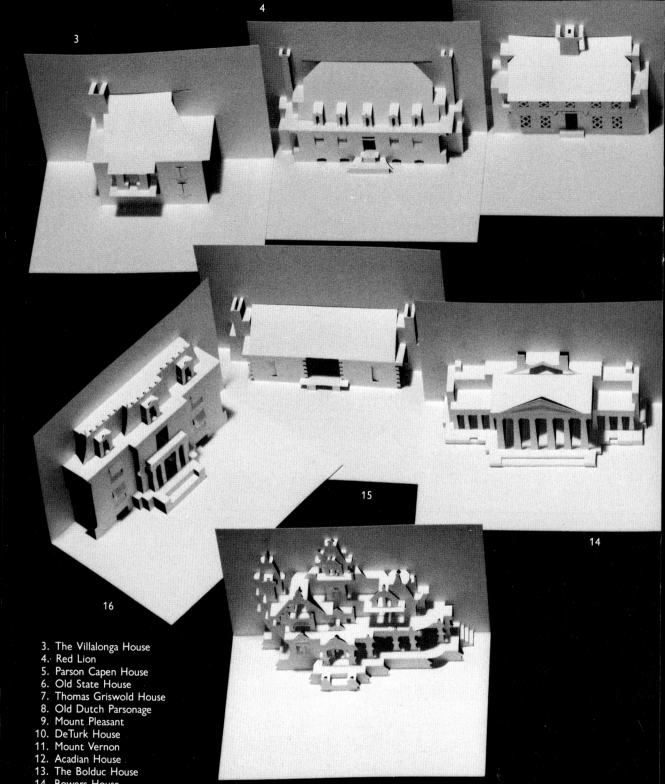

3

4

15

16

14

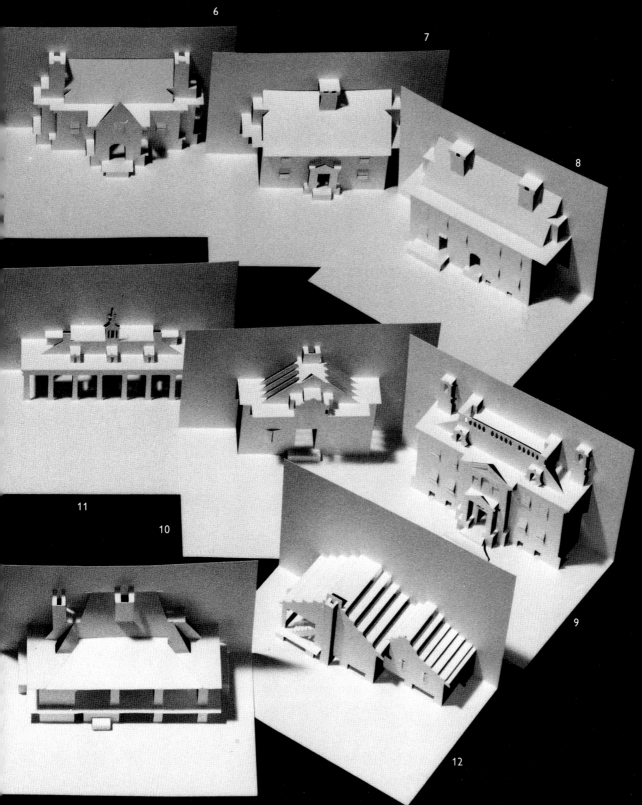

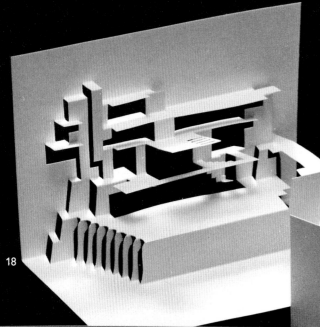

18

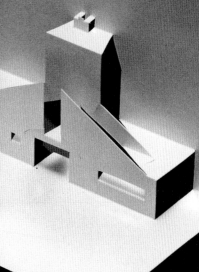

19

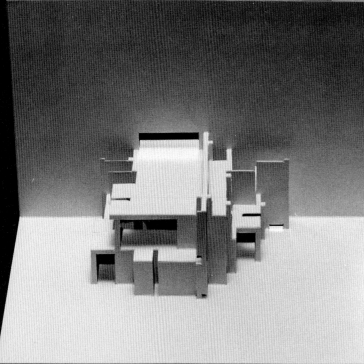

20

18. Fallingwater
19. Vanna Venturi House
20. House VI

Contents

Introduction: A Pop-up Kind of Diversity

One of the aims of Masahiro Chatani's new book is to call attention to the diversity of national and cultural origins in the building traditions of the United States. This variety, striking in itself, may appear all the more remarkable from the point of view of an alert observer belonging to a society as homogeneous as Japan's. Accordingly, the examples chosen—from among many—for this book afford a view of the American dwelling which, though comprehensive, is charmingly individualistic.

How does the cut-and-fold medium of origami architecture exert its attraction and why does it succeed? What, in short, is its fascination?

First of all, like so much that is Japanese it delights in the play of suggestion. Likewise, the diversity of the American heritage defies simplification. This is because of the way it shows forth the future, and the fact that our ethnohistoric diversity furnishes the essential dynamics of present-day world culture. Or, it may be that the reductionism built into Chatani's modeling technique compels a synthesis. With the disappearance nowadays of most constructional limitations, architecture itself is rarely forced to be truly selective of themes and means. There remains, by contrast, in origami architecture a residue of structural process—in short, a form of discipline.

As an approach with its own set of rules, origami inclines to speculation on the sources of diversity, but its gentle interrogation of the past entails less risk than the draftsman's balloon-framed and two-by-foured architecture of a decade ago now commonly offered up as Postmodern classicism. In a way that is ingenious and constructive, origami recycles building ideas and styles; it constitutes an analogous architecture, which can be folded up and put away, in direct contrast with much current production. The latter dulls sensibilities just at the time when a deeper resonance and a finer tuning are wanted.

Origami architecture can simply overlook the blurring of distinctions that are an inevitable feature of late twentieth-century culture. By cutting away, it offers clear, undiluted forms, as opposed to the blending or "styling" at work behind consumer-oriented architecture. It proffers, so to speak, a soft image with a hard edge. Like traditional origami, it does this without impinging on the claims of reality—or of the built environment.

The examples in this book direct attention to the cultural gain that has accrued from the new historical consciousness in contemporary architecture. Negatively put, what is sometimes referred to as the "new historicism" has risen upon the ruins of the drive to conformity expressed in modern architecture. Yet Postmodernism—as the name of a movement and not just a dilemma—is little more than a parody of this situation. Origami reduces the best of both forces to a paper-bound universe operative and stable within the strict limits governed by its techniques. It is a world as little concerned ideologically with a straightforward modernism as with the whistling-in-the-dark of the neo-historicists.

Whence did this diversity arise? Chatani divides the roots into native American, the colonizing influences of Spain, England, France, Holland, and Germany, plus various eclectic and, ultimately, Postmodern embroiderings. Each is offered with his own modest commentary. He makes no attempt to justify his choices. The emphasis is on the *typical* and upon assimilation, such being the aspects that an older culture most clearly perceives in the rapid and heterogeneous evolution of a younger one.

The playfulness of origami as a speculative and formalistic exercise depends for its success on the eye and the hand at work behind it. Both afford that element of sensibility in design that has been dropped from much of real architecture recently, as nearly always occurs at moments when eclecticism gains the field. No doubt, the concern for the authenticity of his own métier fed Chatani's fascination for America's diversified architectural heritage. In contrast to both the international baroque idiom that in Europe preceded American developments as well as the international *modern* style which followed them, Chatani would appear to regard each selection here as an artifact. He views every one as authentic and self-sufficient in its own right, rather than as elements of a procession of socially determined styles. This is evident (and will be still clearer as each house is worked through and set up in its origami representation) despite the emphasis of the commentaries which is laid on continuity of theme and building purpose. The result is to dramatize the uniqueness of every building, as well as highlight the contribution each made in a land where no unified tradition has ever dominated architecture.

In these respects, it is of particular significance that native American house types are here presented on a par with European-style dwellings. For, both the tepee and the pueblo were landmark developments in the architecture of the North American continent. The evolution of the pueblo is believed to be a product of the gradual changeover from cave to pit dwellings in a period corresponding to the early part of the Christian era. One striking form the pueblo dwelling took was a finely worked masonry of sliverlike stones. At the end of the so-called Great Pueblo Period, contemporary with the beginnings of the Gothic style in Europe, some of these lithic apartmentlike complexes were removed once again into the shelter of remote overhanging cliff faces. Further south, the pueblo communities of relatively modern times, like that at Taos (shown here)—despite their impressiveness and beauty—are sometimes referred to as Regressive Pueblos. In a region where no sandstone was to be had, they stood solidly on open ground, innocent of masonry techniques. Before the coming of the Spaniards, the adobe walls of such houses were laboriously built up by hand. The origami model can, of course, only begin to indicate the massive, sculpted quality of these grand architectural ensembles, but it goes a long way in expressing the sense of the Pueblo community as a whole.

Quite unlike these Indian tribes of the Upper Rio Grande, who lived by agriculture, inhabitants of the Plains region were nomadic. They evolved a tent-like habitation which grew out of the conical or domed structures once found throughout the northern half of our continent. The Algonquin term "wigwam" denotes such forerunners, whose frame of wood was normally left standing in place for the life of the dwelling. In the owner's absence during hunting or foraging expeditions, the covering of skins, bark, or matting was, however, removed.

In fact, it is believed that the Plains tribes began their wanderings in earnest only after the introduction of the horse from Spain, when the Indians redesigned the tent to suit their new way of life. It became completely portable in spite of the fact that its poles now extended up to twenty-five feet in length, as opposed to the maximum fifteen-foot length that dogs could be expected to draw in the days before buffalo hunting increased and agriculture declined as a way of life.

Among the colonizers Spain was the earliest to leave a mark on the architecture of the New World. In fact, although the West is the territory we think of most readily in terms of Spanish influence, a number of other settlements and outposts had already been established before the Spaniards reached California. For example, St. Augustine in northeastern Florida was founded in the second half of the sixteenth century. In terms of architecture, the impressive Castillo de San Marcos fortress and, of later date, the Catholic cathedral remain.

Any knowledge of early dwellings is far sketchier. These began as huts of wood and palmetto thatch. Later a kind of concrete using seashell and sand evolved which was to give St. Augustine an Andalusian air—continuous facades abutting the street. Their eleven-inch mortar walls concealed patios which, as these contained a well and garden, were the center of each household. Meanwhile, verandahs were constructed to give a view of the street. Fireplaces with chimneys are thought to have been an innovation inspired by the brief period of British rule (1763–83), as are the glass-paned windows and protective shutters.

The foundation of St. Augustine, plain as the town surely was at its inception, anticipated by nearly half a century permanent English-speaking settlements farther north. Jamestown, in Virginia, was the earliest of these, and its original wooden buildings were prey to the ravages of both damp and fire. It was the latter that caused transfer of the colonial capital to Williamsburg in Bruton Parish in 1699. Official Williamsburg was of brick, though wooden residences probably still predominated. The Red Lion Inn of 1730 is solidly Georgian in its economical use of brick. It relies for architectural effect almost entirely on well-ordered proportions.

Though only fifty years earlier, the Parson Capen House of 1683 at present-day Topsfield, in Massachusetts, lay in the territory settled by dissenters from the English church. It is, thus, a far more austere building. The parsonage is framed in massive timber with an unarticulated exterior of weatherboarding, architecturally restrained except for its medieval jettying, a feature whose purpose remains unknown. Although touched with a vernacular-like simplicity, this Puritan faith became the state religion of the Massachusetts Bay colony. Massachusetts was successfully run on a more or less local basis (not ruled in absentia from London), and it was intended originally that houses be no more than half a mile from the village green that contained the meeting house, with a parsonage nearby. Even the term "church" was not tolerated, such was the Puritan insistence upon plainness. Today only one such meeting house survives, and that in eighteenth-century form: the Old Ship Meeting House at Hingham. It is coeval with Parson Capen's house, and in their essentials the buildings resemble one another.

By the later 1680s, Anglicans too were permitted citizenship in the domain of New England, and it came to pass that Puritan taste reverted to the mainstream. Therefore, Georgian and Puritan elements were frequently combined, whether in ecclesiastical or residential architecture. Meanwhile, in the Middle Colonies both urban Dutch brick and German Palatinate stone rural building traditions flourished. In the Old Dutch Parsonage, shown in rear view by Chatani, brick was actually brought from Holland itself, and in Pennsylvania local stone gave amplitude and solidity to various modes of architectural expression. By the eighteenth century Philadelphia was the largest metropolis, after London, anywhere in the British dominions, with the prosperity of its citizens translated into a rich and full version of prevailing Georgian standards of taste. Thus, Mount Pleasant, just outside the city, is among the grandest and most astonishing of all pre-Revolutionary American houses. The pedimented entry that dominated the main facade of the Old Dutch Parsonage, in adjacent New Jersey, here breaks forward to form a separate pavilion. This encompasses a Serlian window above an elaborate Tuscan portico enframing an arched doorway borne on rusticated piers. The house is set over a tall half-basement and framed with brick quoining articulated to resemble masonry, and surmounted by a balustraded hipped roof flanked by two quadruple chimneys. Finally, an unusual practice in the northern colonies: the main block of the residence is set off by double dependencies in the Palladian manner.

By virtue of its occupant-architect, who, like the emperors of Rome, was known as the "Father of the Country," Mount Vernon, in Virginia, is one of the chief shrines of American domestic architecture. Its Palladianism is expressed in lighter materials than the stone, brick, and stucco of Mount Pleasant. Here wood is carved to resemble stone courses and rendered white. The walls convey an impression of marblelike brilliance owing to glistening particles of sand embedded in the painted surface. Washington's house was significant for the development of an architectural idiom among the landowning classes of the westward-expanding South. In the course of the antebellum agricultural buildup of this part of the country, neo-Palladian vocabulary also met French influences. Of these Chatani gives two somewhat specialized examples of largely local and rural import belonging to the late eighteenth century in the Louisiana territory of France. More striking was the metropolitan architecture of New Orleans itself, whose influence, in the South at least, merged after the Civil War with that of the French Second Empire, represented in this book by the Governor's Mansion at Jefferson City, Missouri. This dignified example restrainedly echoes the bombastic combinations of what in the United States is also known as the General Grant style.

The new nation, however, was already well into revivalism by the earlier nineteenth century, as evidenced by the magnificence of the Joseph Bowers House (1825) at Northampton, Massachusetts. Its architect was Ithiel Town, who had trained in Boston but practiced in New York from 1826 onward. He originally made a name for himself as the foremost bridgebuilder in the country, with a truss called after him, which was also the source of his fortune. Known for his neo-Gothic church spires—as well as exercises like the Bowers House in Greek Revival—he was also the possessor of the finest and largest architectural library in the United States. In more remote areas the Greek Revival existed side-by-side with humble log cabins, like the Issac Parker House. This dwelling dates from three years after Texas statehood (1845), but Houston had as many as twenty such cabins by 1828, while, further east, cabins and temple-fronted public buildings rose virtually cheek by jowl. One thinks of Town and Davis's own North Carolina State Capitol at Raleigh, or Strickland's Tennessee State Capitol at Nashville.

It was this logic of contrasts, still readable at the end of the Federal period, but rampant and mediocre by the close of the century, which led Frank Lloyd Wright to devise a revolutionary type of dwelling, the so-called Prairie House. Though not illustrated here, it is recalled by the inclusion of Wright's atypical, indeed unique, Fallingwater. For Wright, modern architecture stood for a final triumph over useless and hypocritical aesthetic pretensions. It was to be the resolute expression of a democracy in harmony with Nature as well as Wright's own vision of technology. However, style never stands still. For in the end it seems a combination of the old Puritanism and the individualistic do-it-yourself eclecticism of colonial vernaculars has succeeded modernism itself. Today we have, instead of Wright's contemporary once-and-for-all harmonious and balanced equation, the Puritan-like austerity of a Talmudically inspired rationalist in Eisenman, and the rhetorical neo-Neoclassicism of an Italian-American such as Venturi. Despite all theories, and for better or worse, this—and not only to the origamic eye—is where for the moment the cultural diversity of the American architectural heritage has led. Like Eisenman's House VI, Chatani's offerings are clearly "the record of a process."

D. S.

1.
Tepee

c. 1550

Indian City U.S.A.
P.O. Box 695
Anadarko, Oklahoma 73005

On Highway 9, 2 miles south of Anadarko.

When man first began to seek overnight shelter, he had to settle for whatever protection he could find beneath trees or rocks, or perhaps in natural caves. In the vital struggle against the elements, early humans learned to wrap themselves in animal skins for warmth, and it may be assumed that it was not long before someone discovered that the same animal hides used for clothes, if draped over branches or a simple frame construction, could make an effective and portable shelter. This, the birth of the tent—or some similar scenario—no doubt represents a chapter in the history of human dwellings.

Most American Indian tribes, with the exception of the agrarian people in the south and the fishing cultures of the Pacific Coast region, were nomadic hunting-and-gathering societies whose way of life required temporary shelter, and for this purpose the most common dwelling type was the portable tent structure known collectively as the "wigwam."

Among the Plains Indians, the tepee—a word which in the Sioux language simply means "house"—evolved as a more specialized form of this general type. In "setting up house" in any new campsite, the tribal chief's first responsibility was to determine the geomantic aspects of the site and to identify whatever omens were present. Following this, in just a matter of minutes the basic framework of poles would be erected, and in less than a quarter of an hour the outer covering would be in place (this latter task, by the way, was considered "woman's work").

An interior lining was often stretched across the inner surfaces of the poles, creating a layer of air that helped to insulate against the cold; this lining also acted as a secondary rain barrier, and performed still another protective role—that of preventing anyone outside from seeing the fire-lit silhouettes of the people inside.

During heavy rainfall a storm hood one yard in diameter was mounted over the apex, with a small opening on the downwind side of the hood to allow smoke from the firepit to pass through. The tepee indeed functioned very efficiently in many ways as a dwelling place, and when the time came to move it could be swiftly packed up.

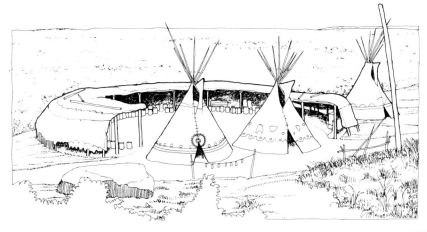

2.
Taos Pueblo

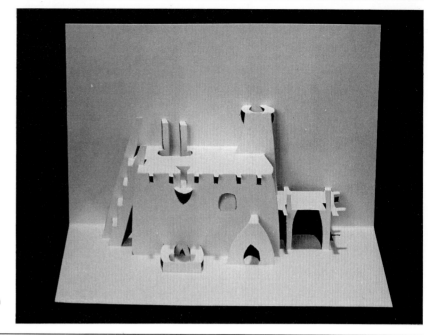

c. 1350

P.O. Box 1846
Taos, New Mexico 87571

2½ miles north of Taos; about 70 miles north of Santa Fe.

Pueblo communities were scattered over the southwest region between the Colorado River and the Rio Grande, with the approximate center of distribution near what is now known as the Four Corners, the meeting point of the states of Colorado, New Mexico, Arizona, and Utah.

The example shown here—the Taos Pueblo—is representative of the pueblo type found from about 1350 to 1750. The Taos Pueblo is situated between an open plain and a narrow stream flowing down from a sacred mountain (here visible in the background). The pueblo complex is a composition of stepped-back forms up to five stories in height, with the oldest houses on the north side of the central plaza and the newer ones facing them from the south, giving the complex a villagelike atmosphere.

The buildings are constructed of sun-dried adobe bricks. Adobe has actually been in use in several parts of the world for thousands of years, especially in areas with dry climates. The American Indians, too, had been using adobe, but it was not until the arrival of the Spaniards that the Indians learned to make molded, sun-dried bricks.

Roofs were constructed of rows of horizontal pine logs overlaid with small rafters and covered with earth, resulting in a flat roof surface. At present, most houses have doors and windows built into the walls, but originally entry was through a hole in the roof. This arrangement was designed to thwart such invaders as the warlike Apache hunters and the nomadic Navajo. With only rooftop access, ladders could easily be withdrawn, a simple but effective method of protection. Today, exterior ladders are still used as a means of access to the upper-level dwellings.

Incidentally, the earthen houses of the pueblo, cool in summer and warm in winter, correspond closely to contemporary ideas of energy conservation.

3.
The Villalonga House

1815–20 (original structure)
mid-1970s (reconstructed)

72 St. George Street
St. Augustine, Florida 32085

North of the intersection of St. George and
Hypolita streets; next to the Columbia Res-
taurant in the center of the Restoration Area.

In 1513, Ponce de Leon, in search of the Fountain of
Youth, landed near the site of modern St. Augustine. He
claimed the territory for Spain, and in less than half a
century St. Augustine had grown into a full-fledged
town.

After 1588, when the powerful Spanish Armada was
defeated by the British Navy, Spain's power and influence
began to fade. In the American Southwest and at St.
Augustine, however, some deeply rooted features of
Spanish culture still remain.

Preservation efforts have restored St. Augustine's historic district to a condition that suggests the general
appearance of the buildings and townscape up through
the mid-eighteenth century.

During the earliest period of settlement, simple construction techniques were borrowed from the local
Seminole Indian tribes, whose dwellings consisted of
wooden-pole frames covered by a woven palm-frond
thatch, for both roof and walls. Thatch was later replaced
with wooden siding, and walls were constructed of stone
with a white plaster finish—at last taking on the look of
true Spanish architecture.

The roofing was cypress-bark thatch, a material which
weathers naturally into variegated shades of gray. In the
interior courts of many houses, the two-story wooden
porch attached to the foot-thick stone walls of the main
structure provides a shaded space with a cool, fresh, and
open feeling.

4.
Red Lion

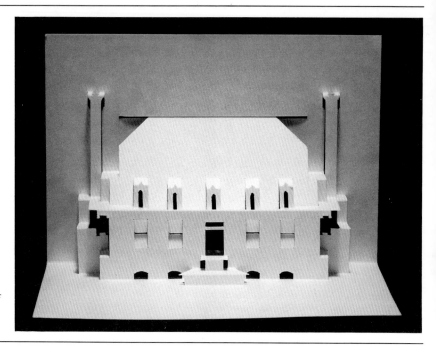

c. 1737 (original structure)
1938 (reconstructed)

Duke of Gloucester Street
Williamsburg, Virginia 23185

On the main pedestrian thoroughfare of
Colonial Williamsburg, past Chowings Tavern
and before the capitol.

Sir Francis Drake's circumnavigational voyage of the globe (1577–80) was an early stimulus for English settlement abroad. In 1606, organized by London backers who had obtained a special charter from James I, a mission of 144 crew and passengers set out in three ships, among them the *Discovery*, bound for the as-yet-unclaimed territory between Spanish-settled Florida and the French colonies in Canada. Reaching land in 1607, they founded the settlement of Jamestown, named in honor of the king. Thirty-nine of the original voyagers had died at sea, and in less than two years' time the severe hardships encountered on land had reduced them to a mere thirty-eight.

By 1625, however, Jamestown was protected by a palisade, and settlers had begun branching out into other areas. Williamsburg developed in the early 1630s and became the capital of Virginia in 1699. The town continued to flourish until 1780 when the capital was moved to Richmond. Restoration of Williamsburg's historic dis-

trict began in 1926, and today it ranks among the world's largest outdoor architectural museums.

The Red Lion is a brick townhouse which first served as an inn for plantation owners who came to participate in Williamsburg's regional congress. It was constructed in 1737 in the prevailing English Georgian style, which evolved during the period of the reconstruction that followed the Great Fire of London in 1666.

The Red Lion's design did not follow Georgian models in all respects, however: the roof, midway in the shift between the older gable-roof style and the neo-Palladian-esque hip-roof style, is a "hipped gable"—with the top half of each gable end cut away by a sloped plane peaking at the ridge—and the tall chimney forms have a stepped-back profile reminiscent of Tudor styles. In addition, the main floor level is elevated, giving this otherwise modestly scaled house a more imposing appearance than many of its colonial contemporaries.

5.
Parson Capen House

1683

Howlet Street
Topsfield, Massachusetts 01983

Near the northeast corner of Topsfield
Common.

The second English settlement in the New World was founded in the year 1609 in Bermuda, two years after Jamestown (see facing page). A third group of English settlers, the 101 Pilgrim Fathers who came in 1620 aboard the *Mayflower*, sailed by way of Holland after fleeing the persecution of the Church of England. As these newcomers were all church separatists whose goal was to follow a pure faith of their own, they had no desire to join the earlier English settlement at Jamestown, which was still affiliated with the official state church. Thus to avoid the Church, these Pilgrim voyagers chose as their destination a point one hundred miles to the north. The place they actually landed, however, was farther north than had been intended—at the point now known as Plymouth Rock, near Cape Cod. It was there at Plymouth that the first *permanent* English colony took root.

Ten years later, however, with the backing of the Church of England's Puritans, four ships and five hundred passengers sailed into what is now known as Boston Harbor to establish a true "Crown Colony," intended as the official center of New England.

Twenty-two miles northeast of Boston, near the town of Topsfield, the landscape is one of age-old meadows with low hills and great hardwood trees, and the picturesque old Parson Capen House in this setting calls to mind an image of the dawn of New England.

The second floor of this three-story house projects out sixteen inches beyond the first-floor wall on the entrance facade, increasing the size of the upper rooms. This overhang is one of the characteristics of the so-called jettied house style favored by the yeomanry of the English Tudor Period (1495–1558).

The first floor consists of two large rooms flanking a massive central chimney with hearth openings over eight feet wide. One of these rooms was the parlor, where the parson carried out his duties, and the other room functioned as a combination kitchen/family room. A steep staircase leads up to bedrooms on the second and third floors.

Sturdy, practical, and austere, the house both inside and out gives one the impression of being thoroughly Puritan in spirit.

6.
Old State House

1676 (original structure)
1934 (reconstructed nearby)

MAILING ADDRESS
Historic St. Marys City
P.O. Box 39
St. Marys City, Maryland 20686

Off Route 5 South, about 2 hours by car from
Washington, D.C.

St. Marys City was founded by English settlers in 1634 and served from 1676 to 1694 as the provincial capital. Today this historic role seems belied somewhat by the town's quiet rural setting on the tip of a peninsula between Chesapeake Bay and the Potomac River. The Old State House, constructed in 1676 as the first capitol, had a single large hall on the first floor which was used initially for governmental assemblies and later for church services as well. The building was torn down in 1829 and its bricks were used instead in the construction of another building, Trinity Church. The present structure is a replica of the original, erected in 1934 to commemorate the tricentennial of the state's founding.

Known as a "cross house" because of its cross-shaped plan, this type of building was derived from traditional English prototypes. Almost invariably, the earliest houses began as one-room dwellings but were soon expanded to include an additional room. For the sake of privacy, a central front-to-back passageway space was introduced later to separate these principal rooms; in order to make this change, however, it was necessary to abandon the idea of using back-to-back fireplaces with a shared central chimney and to move the two chimneys out to the gable ends. With the addition of an enclosed entry at one end of the passageway and a stairwell at the other end, the whole took on the shape of a cross.

The Old State House is close in form and scale to a simple English parish church, but some cross houses were designed on a much grander scale—such as the famous Arthur Allen House, a colonial seat built in Virginia in 1655. Many variations of the cross-plan house can still be seen today in both Virginia and Maryland.

7.
Thomas Griswold House

c. 1774

171 Boston Street
Guilford, Connecticut 06437

About 10 miles east of New Haven, off Exit 58
of I-95.

If it were fair to identify the "generic house" as a historical building type, the Thomas Griswold House would be a prime example. Its general appearance matches the basic image of "house" as perceived by young children—the image they draw at school regardless of the type of house they actually live in. All of the essential homelike features are there: a simple horizontal block form with a central doorway and a symmetrically arranged pattern of windows, surmounted by a pitched, gabled roof with a chimney in the center.

This prototypical generic house emerged in mid-seventeenth-century England as the middle class's best effort at rising to the example of the great manor houses. By the first half of the eighteenth century this dwelling type was in widespread use in the American colonies, though largely devoid of the stylistic refinements that had by that time developed in England. But the relative simplicity of the typical American version should not be attributed solely to inferior economic status or technique; the austerity was intentional, a clear outward expression of the Puritan view of life.

Despite the prescribed plainness, ornament was not altogether absent. For whatever reason—religious, social, or otherwise—special decorative treatment was standard for the doorways not only of residences but sometimes of religious meetinghouses as well, and the Griswold House is no exception. The multipaneled door is flanked by carved flat pilasters and capped by a modest triangular pediment; all of the ornamentation is concentrated here, and no other decorative details are to be found on the exterior.

The Griswold House does differ from the hypothetical generic prototype in one respect: it has a rear lean-to addition and an asymmetrically extended roof, the rear plane longer and lower than the front.

Although the exterior is now white, it is more than likely that the house, like most wooden houses built in New England during this later period, would have been painted brown, gray, or even a somber red or yellow. Authenticity aside, however, the whiteness suggests the notion of purity, which surely had a hand in shaping the character of this house.

8.
Old Dutch Parsonage

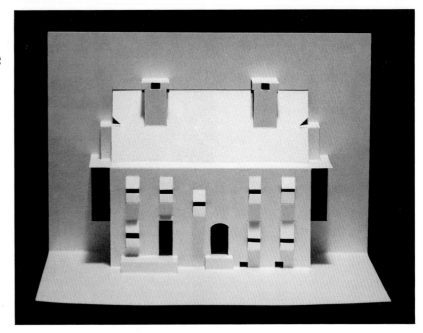

1751

MAILING ADDRESS
38 Washington Place
Somerville, New Jersey 08876

12 miles from New Brunswick; unnumbered
house on Washington Place.

The Old Dutch Parsonage is a quiet, massive structure of brick standing against a wooded backdrop deep in the Raritan Valley, not too distant from the mouth of the Hudson River.

In 1614, the Dutch West India Company founded a New Netherland settlement around the Hudson River in the coastal area now shared by the states of New York and New Jersey. Other settlements soon followed. New York City started out originally as New Amsterdam, and the streetscapes of that period clearly showed the traditional Dutch influence of gable-wall entry facades which were characteristic of Dutch towns then as now. By contrast, the gables in English houses were typically at the sides of the house rather than at the front, and it was thus the broad side of the house which faced the street. The Dutch style prevailed for New Amsterdam's first fifty years, but after the town came under English control in 1664 English architectural fashions came to the fore, and

the gable lost its dominance as a characteristic streetscape feature.

The Old Dutch Parsonage is actually a combination of both Dutch and English styles, with a two-story-high, broad-wall street front topped by a large gable at the center.

It is interesting to note that the bricks used were produced in Holland, which showed not so much the builder's desire to use authentic materials but rather some shipper's need to provide ballast for his otherwise too lightly-loaded ship on the way to pick up cargo in America.

Also of interest is the fact that the first owner of the house, the Reverend John Frelinghuysen, was a member of George Washington's staff. The nearby Wallace House—built in 1778 and occupied by General Washington as his wartime headquarters that same winter—has also been restored.

9.
Mount Pleasant

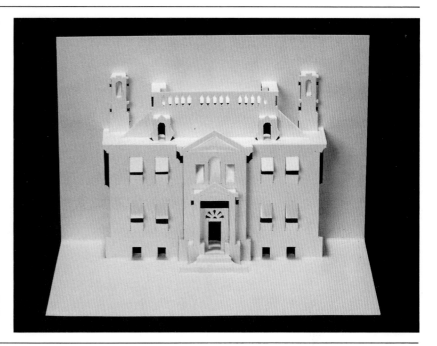

1761

Mount Pleasant Drive
Fairmount Park
Philadelphia, Pennsylvania 19101

Between Fountain Green Drive and Mount Pleasant Drive in Fairmount Park; park headquarters are on 42nd and Parkside.

Philadelphia, America's first planned city, was laid out in 1682 according to designs by William Penn. Prosperity came quickly to the new town and it soon became the effective center of the American colonies, later serving as the young nation's capital from 1790 to 1800.

It was common for wealthy Philadelphians of that period to spend the summer in the nearby countryside along the Schuylkill River, and many fine villas and country mansions were built for that purpose. Following the outbreak of typhoid in 1822, however, all were abandoned, and it was not until the centennial in 1876 that a thorough restoration of the buildings and grounds was carried out (ultimately resulting in the creation of a great city park, the largest in the United States today).

The interiors of some eight such mansions are open to the public, and among these perhaps the most luxurious and elegant is Mount Pleasant. Although the architecture is basically of the Georgian idiom (popular in England throughout the eighteenth century) there is an element of grandeur and display that sets this masterpiece apart. In the entrance facade, the front doorway is framed between curve-edged stairs below and an arched "fanlight" above; this latter embellishment is topped by a pedimented roof which projects slightly, and above this, at the second floor level, is a Palladian window. The whole is dominated by another, larger pedimented roof. In all, it is a majestic composition.

Finely detailed dormer windows are set into the slopes of the hipped roof, and atop the truncated ridge is what is known as a "captain's walk" or "widow's walk"—a nonfunctional rooftop lookout platform bordered by railings and decorative balustrades. The two tall chimneys—pierced at the top with slender arched side-wall openings—dominate the ends of the facade.

The accessory buildings reinforce the symmetrical composition of the facade. These two structures—a servants' quarters and a kitchen-house—were in most respects designed in the same style as the main building, although the roof shapes do differ. Mount Pleasant is notable for other reasons as well, but certainly the overall unity of the main and subsidiary structures provides a pleasing balance of grandeur and simplicity.

10.
DeTurk House
(The Outlooker)

1767

MAILING ADDRESS
Historic Preservation Trust of Berks County
P.O. Box 1681
Reading, Pennsylvania 19603

On DeTurk Road, $\frac{1}{4}$ mile south of Route 73 in
Oley, Berks County; not open to the public,
but can be viewed from the road.

The late seventeenth-century settlements started by William Penn, in the region named Pennsylvania in honor of his father, were originally established by English Quakers. Founded on the premise of religious tolerance, these settlements attracted new immigrants from many parts of Europe.

The earliest houses were of wood, but such buildings were in time outnumbered by sturdy stone structures of a type that seemed to recall the image of traditional medieval-style dwellings, at least in their solidity. One common, if primitive, example was the "bank house," built into a slope, with the main floor entry at grade level and a lower-floor entry below to one side. Thus, half buried in the earth, the lower-level living areas were cool in summer and warm in winter.

The DeTurk House is a typical bank house, displaying additional features common to the times, such as "outlookers." These were wood-framed overhanging roof projections, usually covered with slate. In the front gable wall is an attic door which allowed access to the storage loft via a pulley-hoist used to lift the goods up from the ground level; this door was sheltered by another type of projected overhang in the shape of a gable roof.

The inner surfaces of the window shutters were painted in bright floral-pattern designs. With the shutters in the open position, the painted flowers enlivened the building's exterior, and the same designs provided a colorful contrast to the white-walled interior when the shutters were closed.

Overall, the DeTurk house has the proportions and character of a comfortable medieval-type cottage, and somehow exudes a fairy-tale-like charm.

11.
Mount Vernon

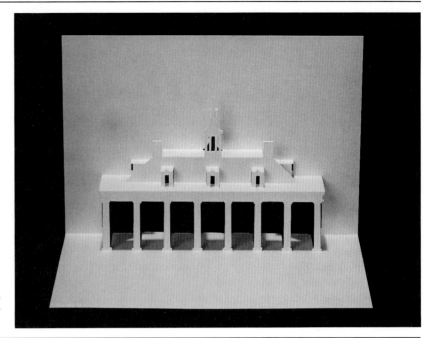

1735 (original structure)
1754 (additions)

Mount Vernon Ladies' Association
Mount Vernon, Virginia 22121

At the end of George Washington Parkway,
15 miles south of downtown Washington,
D.C.

Fifteen miles south of what is now Washington, D.C. is the site chosen by George Washington's father in the mid-1730s for the new family home. Situated on the crest of a gentle slope overlooking the Potomac River, the house was at this period an unimpressive 1½-story structure of vernacular inspiration. In 1740 it became the property of George's half-brother Lawrence, who, in one of history's ironic twists, named the estate after the distinguished military leader Edward Vernon, an admiral in the British Navy.

Two years after Lawrence's death in 1752, the house and property went to George. Around the time of his marriage to the wealthy widow Martha Custis in 1759, he enlarged the house by adding a full second story with attic rooms, and by 1785 the scale had been expanded still further to include two-story extensions to both left and right, a banquet hall in one end and a library in the other. Yet another enlargement added slave-quarter wings at both sides of the main building, while across the river-facade was erected a fourteen-foot-wide, two-story-high "piazza" (or porch). This created in effect a large open-air living room, a space both casual and monumental—an unparalleled gesture of grandeur.

This constant remodeling resumed when Washington returned to Mount Vernon in 1783 after the American Revolution had come to an end. Noteworthy among these later additions is the cupola of the type often seen on official public buildings of an earlier period.

Mount Vernon's evolution may have helped the older English Georgian style evolve into a more characteristically regional idiom that might be called a "planter's federal," thereby adding a new note to the architecture of the new country. In any event, Washington's own plantation, along with Thomas Jefferson's splendid Monticello, has always retained a special place in American heritage.

12.
Acadian House

1700s (original structure)
1820s (remodeled)

1200 North Main Street
St. Martinville, Louisiana 70582

Off LA 31 just north of St. Martinville.

The French were already active on the coast of the new American continent less than ten years after Columbus's arrival. Among the earliest arrivals were commercial fishermen in the area of present-day Nova Scotia, while others later pushed farther inland up the St. Lawrence River to trade with the Indians for furs.

This whole area, now part of southeastern Canada, eventually came to be known as New France. More territory was added to France's holdings late in the seventeenth century, but at a significant distance from the original northern Atlantic coast settlements; this acquisition came about as the result of Robert de La Salle's expedition from Montreal to the mouth of the Mississippi River. Reaching the coast in the spring of 1682, La Salle claimed the entire region for France and gave it the name Louisiana in honor of King Louis XIV.

Nova Scotia—known to the French as Acadie—was ceded to England in 1713, and in 1755 the Acadian French were deported for refusing to take the English oath of allegiance. The Acadians scattered, but one group managed at length to make its way south into France's other American possession, finally settling in the swamplands of Louisiana.

These people—also known as Cajuns—and particularly their direct descendants, the Creoles, typically lived in cabins of a rather particular style. The dwelling was a wooden structure supported by brick piers and raised up off the ground to allow air to circulate beneath the floor. The main body of the house, which contained only one room, had a comfortable porch across the front and a stairway leading directly from outside up to the children's room in the attic. A singular feature was the manner in which the house was added to: it became a linear assembly of single rooms, with door openings lined up for straight-through ventilation. It can easily be imagined that this simple composition was a practical response to the challenge of living in the hot southern climate.

13.
The Bolduc House

1770 (original structure)
c. 1785 (relocated and additions made)

120 South Main Street
Ste. Genevieve, Missouri 63670

60 miles south of St. Louis; on Main Street near Market Street.

Although France had been quick to explore the New World soon after Columbus, it was not until 1732 that they established the town of Ste. Genevieve. It was originally founded as a lead-mining site on the Mississippi River some fifty miles downriver from present-day St. Louis. French control of the area finally came to an end with President Jefferson's Louisiana Purchase in 1803, but a French ambience still lingers on.

The Bolduc House is among those historic buildings contributing to the town's French atmosphere, though the house shows more of a Norman than Parisian influence. Built around 1785, the raised-floor wooden structure rests on a stone foundation; the main beams were recycled from a still earlier house on a nearby site, and the foundation construction method followed the "poteaux-sur-sole" system (posts-on-sill). This consisted of a row of rough-planed log posts set upon the stone sill at close intervals. The wall above was an infill mixture of clay, straw, and animal hair. This system was an improvement upon the "poteaux-en-terre" system (posts-in-earth) used in the 1720s, in which the posts were set directly into the ground.

The exterior walls were finished with a whitewash applied over the various materials—wood, clay, and stone—resulting in a uniform overall texture.

The double-pitched hipped roof, steep in the center and gently pitched over the veranda, was a typical feature of these early French colonial houses. Hand-split wooden shingles now cover the entire roof, but it is likely that the original roofing material, at least for the steep upper portion, would have been grass thatch as in Normandy. As a whole, the forms of the roof and the open veranda give the house a light and airy appearance—somewhat like a tent with raised flaps, or perhaps a hat; indeed this roof shape did later come to be known as a "bonnet roof."

14.
Bowers House

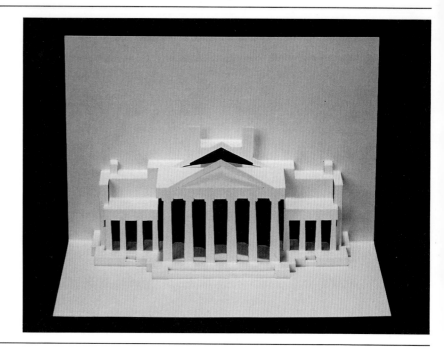

c. 1825

Building torn down in 1915;
historical society (413) 584-6011.

Early-nineteenth-century American architecture owes much to a revived classicism. Although English, and occasional French, architectural influences never really died out, imported vernaculars were displaced in the years following the Revolution when Americans felt compelled to search for a style that they could call their own. During the post-colonial Federal Period (1780–1820) the familiar English Georgian style gave way to a more elaborate neo-classicism as new fashions like the Adam style (Robert Adam, 1728–92) came to the foreground.

American architecture next embarked upon a period of eclecticism, first looking to ancient Greece in a wistful search for models appropriately symbolic of democratic ideals. Athenian temples apparently satisfied this requirement, inspiring the Greek Revival style which quickly spread throughout the country. For most residences, the thick columns and other temple elements were fabricated of wood and painted white in imitation of the classical stone monuments, themselves carved in imi-

tation of the original wooden temple structures of an even earlier age.

For the columns of the Bowers House, the capitals were executed in the graceful spiral-volute Ionic style (rather than in the older, simpler Doric style or in the delicate arabesque patterns of the Corinthian style), possibly in recognition of the fact that, at a large scale at least, the Ionic forms were best suited to both the potential of woodcarving techniques and the limitations of wood itself as a medium.

The facade was intended to impress, and it does. The colonnade continues around the corners and along both sides of the house; three-sided porticoes, however, were not a standard feature of authentic Grecian temples.

This grand colonnade, two stories in height, was intended to amplify the three-dimensionality of the whole and create a buffer space between outside and inside, if only a visual one, unlike the "piazza" at Mount Vernon of some years before.

15.
Parker Cabin

1848

Log Cabin Village
2222 West Rosedale
Forth Worth, Texas 76110

At the intersection of University Drive and
Log Cabin Village Lane; across from Forest
Park Zoo.

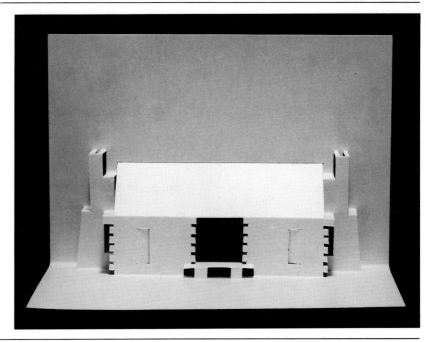

One symbol of early America and the new frontier is the rustic log cabin. This humble dwelling type was home for pioneer settlers throughout the breadth of the eastern United States, and among those who were born in or who lived in log cabins were seven presidents. But the log cabin, however much a part of America's historical identity, was not of American origin. This type of log construction was used in various parts of Europe, and the Swedes were said to have been the first to employ it in the New World, around 1638. New Sweden, concentrated along the Delaware River and covering portions of present-day Pennsylvania, New Jersey, and Delaware, was in fact short-lived—lasting in name a mere seventeen years—but the legacy of the log cabin was permanent.

The Parker Cabin is one of six meticulously restored nineteenth-century log cabins clustered in a small village setting in Fort Worth, Texas. Though all were constructed using similar techniques and were built during the same general period (1848–70), the designs vary both in style and scale. The simplest, like the prototypical form of any dwelling type, is a tiny one-room house. Other standard variations include two-room single-story structures and two-story structures. Yet another type, the so-called dogtrot house, features a somewhat more unusual composition: under a single roof stand two discrete rooms separated by an open-ended breezeway space (this was supposedly where the dogs slept—hence the name "dogtrot").

The Parker Cabin belongs to this last type. Built in 1848 by soldier-statesman Isaac Parker (1793–1884), it contains a kitchen/dining space in one "wing" and a combination living room/sleeping quarters in the other; for warmth, each wing has its own fireplace and chimney. The central area served not only as a passageway but also as an open-air living room/workroom, a highly useful addition to the otherwise small dwelling space. One may wonder why in fact this passage was not enclosed since it was already fully sheltered by the roof and already provided with a floor, but in any case the disposition of space seems to have been most pleasantly arranged.

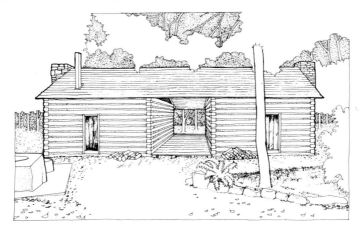

16.
Governor's Mansion

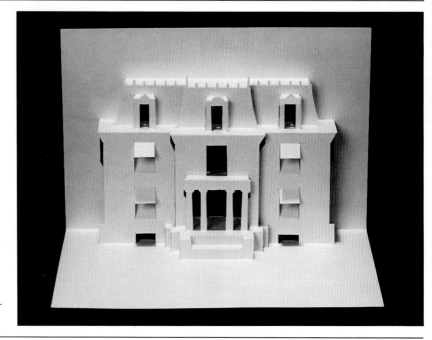

1871

100 Madison Street
Jefferson City, Missouri 65101

North of Highway 50 (Jefferson City Express-
way).

President Thomas Jefferson, after concluding the purchase of the Louisiana Territory from France in 1803,
took part in an expedition to explore some of the newly
acquired domain. One of the points where Jefferson's
party landed, on the banks of the Missouri, was later
named Jefferson City in his honor; it was designated as
the state capital when Missouri became the twenty-
fourth state of the union.

The governor's official residence was constructed just
as American architecture was entering an increasingly
eclectic phase (1860–1930), with the style of the French
Second Empire coming into vogue all across the country.
The previous two decades in Paris had seen a momen-
tous transformation as Napoleon III, through the designs
of his planning deputy, Baron Eugène Georges Hauss-
mann (1809–91), rearranged the patterns of the city's life
by creating a network of grand boulevards. As attention
was drawn toward this new image of Paris, one distinctive
feature of the Parisian streetscape stood out: the profile

of the ubiquitous mansard roof. This feature, popular-
ized two centuries earlier by architect Francois Mansart
(1598–1666), became a dominant theme in America's
public building architecture—a fairly typical example of
which is this governor's mansion.

Although the original idea of the mansard roof may
have been to steal more space at the attic level, its true
appeal in the States was probably due more to its palatial
character and hint of Parisian charm.

The composition is indeed distinctive, with the steeply
pitched roof starting upward from the cornice in a steep
concave arc; stately pedimented dormers are set into this
subtly undulating plane, and the upper edge is ornament-
ed all around with cast-iron roof cresting.

By the late 1880s the general characteristics of the
mansard roof had found their way into various rival
eclectic idioms, such as High and Late Victorian, and for
several more decades traces of Old Paris could still be
seen in American town halls and private residences.

MOUNT PLEASANT

9

Level A

········ mountain fold   ---- valley fold   ———— cutting line

In this house, featured on the cover, the doorway is the centerpiece of the whole, so particular care should be taken with this and the two front steps. Half-cut both mountain and valley folds so that the steps are crisp and neat.

17.
The Carson Mansion

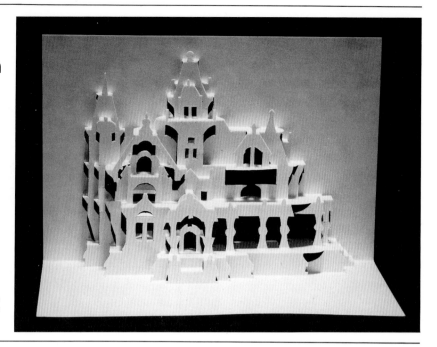

1884–5 (original structure)
1952 (additions)

143 M Street
Eureka, California 95501

Go to Second and L Street, then turn up Second Street toward M Street; not open to public, but can view from road.

More than one hundred carpenters and two years' time were required to create the incomparable Carson Mansion. Fine woods from all over the world were used in the crafting of this exuberant work with its undeniably fairy-tale-like character.

Wherever one finds any mention of Victorian houses in architectural literature the Carson Mansion is almost universally brought forth as America's prime example. The setting, too, is worthy of comment, since this building is an integral part of California's renowned Pacific coast scenery, though the scenic *interior* of this grand eighteen-room mansion is not open to public view.

Ornate design was the hallmark of eclectic High-Victorian architecture in the late nineteenth and early twentieth centuries. Among the many possible stylistic features available to designers during that period, those employed in the Carson House include the following: (1) an asymmetrical facade reminiscent of the Italian villa—at that time the fashion in England as well; (2) an irregular plan, characteristic of Gothic revival plan layouts; (3) a huge tower head with a mansard roof, in the Second Empire style, rising over Venetian Gothic dormers; and (4) a Queen-Anne-style porch/veranda composition, and Queen Anne tower finials and gable ornaments.

In general, the house might most aptly be described as a "picturesque Eastlake-style eclectic Victorian villa." Charles L. Eastlake, an English art critic, urged in his popular *Hints on Household Taste* (1868) a return to the relative restraint seen in the interiors and furnishings of the Middle Ages, as opposed to the excessive use of Baroque ornamentation which was so much in favor among Eastlake's contemporaries. Eastlake's message somehow missed its mark in America, however; ironically, the architectural style that came to bear his name was influenced not by his writing but by the furniture styles that he promoted in his book, as architects and builders borrowed liberally from the forms and motifs of the furniture illustrated in the book and simply reproduced them at a larger scale on the house exterior.

The Carson House was a jubilant response to a romantic client's dream. To reflect now on the currents of romanticism that inspired the architecture of a century ago may help shed some light on the currents of today.

18.
Fallingwater

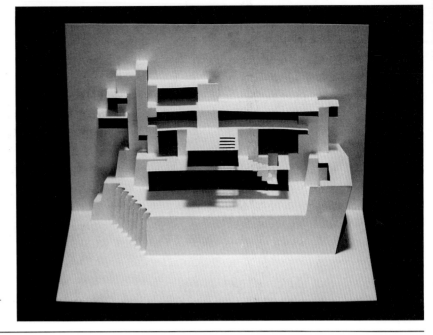

1936

P.O. Box R
Mill Run, Pennsylvania 15464

On Pa. Route 381, 70 miles southeast of Pittsburgh.

One of America's most celebrated examples of harmony between architecture and nature is Frank Lloyd Wright's Fallingwater in its woodland setting alongside—and over—the Bear Run Waterfall in rural Pennsylvania, near Pittsburgh. As many have observed, part of the magic of this harmonious bond is that the building does not appear to melt *into* the surroundings but rather to grow *out* of them. The vertical elements, the walls rising up out of the ground, are of natural materials—rough-textured flat-coursed stone—but the series of horizontal planes and "trays" that project out away from those walls are all of smooth, cream-white concrete, not at all "natural" in themselves but instead distinctly manmade, emphasizing both by form and by finish the fact that this *is* a human artifact and that nature is simultaneously its domain and its means of support.

Wright's ability to fuse the interior and exterior is in abundant evidence here. It is seen not only in the openness afforded by the almost unbroken band of windows and by the clear glass skylights but also in the continuity achieved by the use of identical materials both inside and out. The viewer's eye can follow the surfaces of the walls or floor straight out beyond the glass and into the space of the terraces. The terraces themselves seem to reach out into the scenery, extending more than halfway across the narrow stream—close enough to touch the branches of the trees on the opposite bank. While out on one of these daringly cantilevered balconies it is not difficult to imagine oneself floating—but whether on water or on air, does not really matter.

Even though all of the main interior spaces face toward the stream side, the water is much easier to hear than to see. But Wright has made sure that the stream is not out of reach in practical terms: he has provided a stairway leading directly down to a platform which hovers just above the water's surface. The stairs give the interior space yet another direction of focus—downward, in addition to upward and outward—contributing one more compositional link between building and site.

It goes without saying that to make the best use of the natural features of the site is one of the essentials of architecture. But to meet this challenge and to succeed so well—as Wright did at Fallingwater—is indeed something very rare.

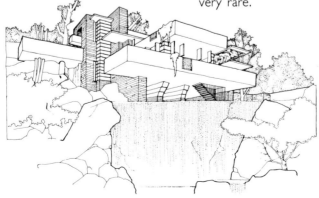

19.
Vanna Venturi House

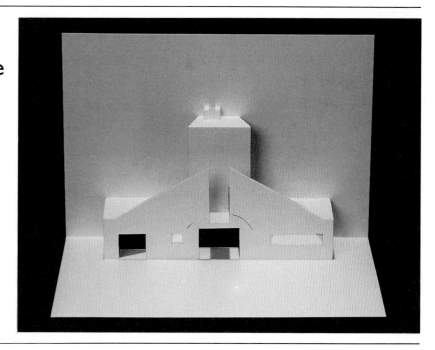

1961 (designed)
1965 (built)

Chestnut Hill
Philadelphia, Pennsylvania

Private residence.

Architect Robert Venturi's maiden work, the house that he designed for his mother, probably remains his most famous building. But Venturi's fame and influence have stemmed equally from his 1966 theoretical treatise *Complexity and Contradiction in Architecture.* The book gained instant worldwide attention. Its impact on young architects was profound, and it is responsible in part for the "movement" of architectural Postmodernism. In his criticism of the so-called International Style of the Modernist movement, Venturi pointed out that by ignoring the value of decoration Modernists had abandoned much of the potential for meaning in architectural expression. Therefore he set out to remind architects of the deep "flavor" latent in the decorative arts.

The house at Chestnut Hill, Pennsylvania, has long since come to be recognized as one of the classic landmarks of Postmodernism, and it is now one of the standard pilgrimage spots for students of architecture. Approaching the house, the visitor at once confronts the entire width of the facade—a broad gable, split down the middle and dominated by a large central chimney. In effect the image is that of a grand European manor house which is roughly—and ironically—translated into the modest terms of a middle-class American family dwelling. The entrance loggia, a comfortably-scaled rectangular opening, is capped by an applied wooden molding (said to be a rain diverter) which is curved to suggest an arch; this arch form is there to serve as a symbol of a formal entranceway, and the fact that there actually is no arch and that no structural purpose is being served is, according to Venturi, irrelevant in terms of Postmodern architectural vocabulary as long as the *significance of entry* itself is clearly expressed. In the eyes of the Modernists, however, the use of such elements as gables and arches had long been scorned as unsophisticated and impossible to account for in any rational way.

This building at first glance seems not so extraordinary—just a house of typical woodframe construction and finish, with a symmetrical Palladian-style facade—but after a moment this impression is forgotten as one begins to take note of the asymmetrical treatment of the openings and to assimilate some of the other "complexities and contradictions" in the house's composition. The dynamic rear facade and the subtle spatial articulation of the interior add to the effect of Venturi's new direction in architecture in the 1960s.

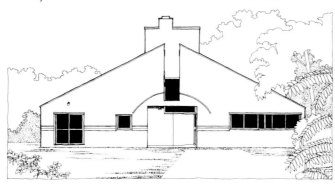

20.
House VI

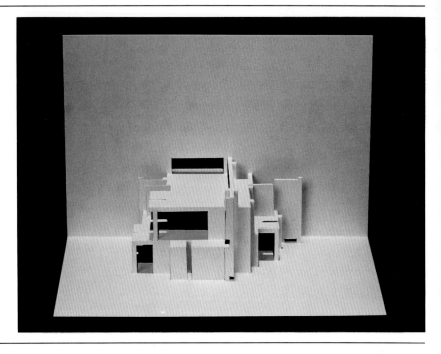

1975
Cornwall, Connecticut
Private residence.

Of the eleven numbered house designs in architect Peter Eisenman's series, only four have been built. Eisenman has attained an unprecedented level of abstraction through the composition methods employed in these designs, all of which have a sculpture-like quality totally devoid of any common reference to "house-ness." Not only is there no sign of tradition or ornament, there is also no logical expression of structure (the articulation of posts, beams, and bearing walls is either intentionally ambiguous or simply nonexistent), no sense of material (for example, the massiveness of stone or the warm texture of wood or brick), and no curves or sloped planes which might suggest an entry arch or an ordinary roof.

With a simple box as the conceptual point of departure, Eisenman's design process manipulates three-dimensional space by dividing and assembling it in a trial-and-error progression—following the rules of whatever pure intellectual game he has chosen as the theme for that particular work—until the resulting physical composition satisfies both visual and conceptual requirements of the theme.

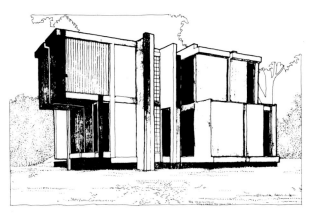

When House I was designed and built in 1968, it was referred to as "cardboard architecture"—applying the same term used to describe some of the works of the great Modernist master Le Corbusier. If one ignores its scale, House I does indeed look like a white paper model. By the elimination of material expression, all surfaces have been reduced to mere "surfaces," enhancing the abstract character of the building.

House VI, built in a wooded area in the Connecticut countryside, has a similarly neutral model-like character despite its concrete construction. The overall composition of spatial volumes and structural elements has been designed into an irregular three-dimensional grid with four- or six-foot horizontal spacing dimensions and eight-foot vertical dimensioning. The grid lines are articulated as a kind of skeletal frame composed of six-inch-square framing members, and this is uniformly expressed throughout—in the floor, wall, or ceiling whether or not the framing member is actually there. In some cases where a beam or a post *should* be, there is instead a slit—even, say, in the middle of the floor in the second-story bedroom. In other words Eisenman's designs contain numerous delightfully incongruous details.

Through various methods, and to varying degrees, Eisenman has abstracted the forms, materials, functions, and meanings of architecture—and inside the resulting physical space he has made provision for enough of the necessities of life to create, nonetheless, the identity and reality of "a house."

General Information

TOOLS

1. RULERS
You should have two rulers, one of clear plastic and another of metal.

2. STYLUS
The stylus was first invented to mark stencil paper. It resembles a pencil, with a metal point instead of a lead. It will be used here to score fold lines and make holes. If a stylus is unobtainable, use a compass or divider to punch holes, and an inkless ball point pen or wooden paperknife to score lines.

3. TWEEZERS
You should choose a pair of tweezers with sharp, pointed ends for grasping small areas, making slight corrections, and other detailed work.

4. SNAP-OFF CUTTER
This or any type of small craft knife with a sharp edge and a pointed tip will work. You should use one you feel comfortable with.

5. UNDERLAY
The underlay may be either thick plastic or cardboard. It serves not only to protect your desk or table but, more importantly, to make the cutting easier.

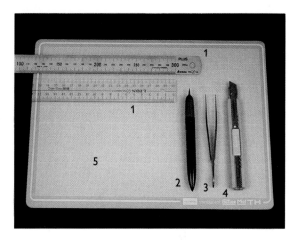

METHOD 1–Using the Original Pattern

Before starting, it is advisable to make a photocopy of the pattern. Not only will this allow you to make additional models at a later date by following Method 2, but the copy will be a useful reference for checking the convex and concave lines as you progress. If you are using the original patterns, you should be advised that the printed lines, though light, will show. The Villalonga House (No. 3) is the example used below.

1. Tear out the pattern page.

2. Make a copy.

3. Place the pattern face up on the underlay, and using the metal ruler trim away excess paper around the borderlines with the cutter.

4. Score the valley folds (concave), which are indicated by −−−. To do this, align the ruler with the line to be scored and press firmly with the stylus, following the ruler's edge.

When there are many small valley folds, turn the paper over and half-cut the lines from the back (see next step). This makes the eventual folding much easier. *Do not half-cut the central valley fold.* This fold should be as strong as possible in order for the card to stand at a 90-degree angle.

| LEVEL OF DIFFICULTY |

There are three levels of difficulty, "A" being the most advanced. The projects in this book are arranged for historical and architectural fluency. For those readers desiring to start from the easier projects and work their way up to the hardest, projects are here grouped according to level:

A—9 · 17 · 18 · 20

B—4 · 5 · 11 · 12 · 13 · 14 · 16

C—1 · 2 · 3 · 6 · 7 · 8 · 10 · 15 · 19

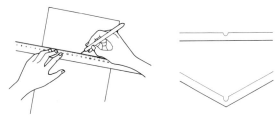

step 4   Score the valley folds.

5. Prepare the mountain folds (convex), which are marked thus: ·······. To do this, align the ruler with the convex line and draw the cutter blade lightly across the paper, cutting no deeper than halfway through. This half-cut will make it easier to fold, and the angle will be sharper and cleaner. Be very careful not to cut too deeply. If you do inadvertently cut through the paper, be sure to repair the cut before folding the card (see Repairs).

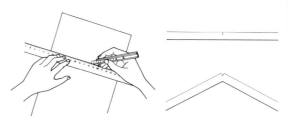
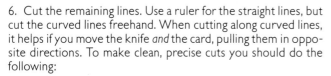

step 5   Half-cut the mountain folds.

6. Cut the remaining lines. Use a ruler for the straight lines, but cut the curved lines freehand. When cutting along curved lines, it helps if you move the knife *and* the card, pulling them in opposite directions. To make clean, precise cuts you should do the following:

- Make sure you press down firmly with the ruler.
- Cut at a right angle to the paper.
- Pass the blade gently over the line two or three times, cutting completely through on the final pass.
- Cut the shorter lines and areas clustered with many lines first, then cut the longer lines.
- When cutting an acute angle, cut toward the tip to get a sharp point (see illustration).

step 6   For acute angles, cut *toward* the corner.

7. When the fold lines and cutting lines have been readied, the real origami begins. With the folding process, unlike the cutting process, you start with the major lines.

Before you begin pushing out the structure, check that you have cut the lines perfectly, according to the pattern. To fold, lift the paper in both hands with the front side facing you, and, from the back, start pushing out the convex folds. The house will begin to emerge. Some parts may not push out easily, probably because the cutting has been insufficient. If this occurs, stop and check the lines. *The folding/pressing out should never be done quickly. Fold slowly, frequently referring to the photograph of the completed card.*

Occasionally, while pushing the form out, some fold lines may be too stiff and resist your attempts to fold them. For mountain folds, return the paper to its flat state and half-cut the problematic lines a little more deeply. On occasion some flat areas may show signs of creasing. When this happens, avoid putting any pressure on that area.

For valley folds: Since each fold is dependent for its shape and strength on every other part of the structure, lightly press all the fold lines again, one by one, especially the center concave fold lines, then try the troublesome fold once more. If necessary, use the tweezers and the tip of the stylus.

step 7   Push out the structure . . .

step 7   folding major lines as you go.

8. To finish, continue to fold carefully until the two halves of the paper can be folded together. Make sure that all lines have been folded, then press the paper down firmly along the center line, completing the card. Press down hard on the structure inside. Open the card to 90 degrees. Open any windows or doors and make any minor adjustments you think are necessary.

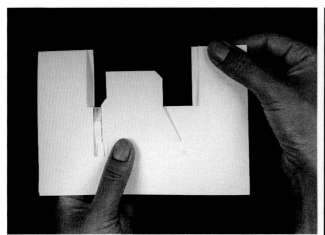

step 8   Fold in half and press the center line.

Completed house.

METHOD 2—Tracing the Pattern

You should use stiff card stock or stiff white paper. Thin paper will simply not result in an effective pop-up card, so paper similar to that of the patterns in this book is recommended.

1. After selecting the paper, you must determine which way the fibers run. When paper is manufactured, the fibers line up in the same direction; the strength of the fold lines will depend on the direction of the line relative to the fibers. To ascertain the direction of the fibers, cut a 2-inch square from the paper you wish to use. If you bend it with two fingers, you will realize very quickly that the paper bends more easily in one direction than in the other. The direction in which it bends most easily is the direction in which the fibers run. The central valley fold of the card should run perpendicular to the direction of the fibers to give the pop-up building strength.

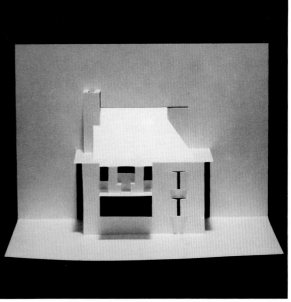

step 1   Test the paper for direction of fibers.

central valley fold

2. Make a copy of the original.

3. Place the stiff paper on the underlay, and lay the copied pattern on top.

4. Using the tip of a stylus or compass, make small holes at every corner or junction where lines meet, starting with the six points around the border of the card. For curved lines, prick many points along the curve. Keeping the two sheets aligned, carefully hold them up to the light to verify that you have marked all the points.

5. The puncture marks will serve as your reference for cutting and building the origami. Referring to the original pattern as often as necessary, proceed according to Method 1 (beginning from step 4).

REPAIRS

When you have cut a fold line by mistake.
Washi (Japanese handmade paper) is highly recommended, but any strong, lightweight white paper can be used to make the repair. Cut the paper into very small pieces, and glue it to the back of the card using a non-waterbased glue. (Waterbased glues cause stiff paper to swell.) This is detailed work, so the tweezers are of immense value.

When a thin strip of paper has weakened and shows signs of creasing.
Using non-waterbased glue, reinforce the weakened area by gluing a fragment of the same type of paper to the back. Make sure it doesn't show from the front.

step 4 Make a hole at every corner.

VARIATIONS

Poster-size: When making a particularly large example, say for an exhibition, the pattern must be replotted on graph paper since the relative lengths of the horizontal and vertical lines will change. To do this, draw a $1/4$-inch square grid over a copy of the original pattern in this book. Draw a larger grid on the larger sheet of paper and redraw the pattern, square by square.

As the size of the card increases, not only must the pattern be adjusted but the thickness of the paper must be increased proportionately.

When you have chosen appropriate paper, do not forget to check the direction of the fibers, as explained in the first step in Method 2.

Miniature-size: For extreme reduction, relative lengths are not affected, so it is possible to use a reduced photocopy. When the scale is smaller, however, the cutting and folding require a much more delicate touch. The drastic reduction in size may also necessitate elimination of a few details.

If small-scale projects intrigue you, you might consider making three-dimensional namecards.

Changing the card size: The cards in this book are all of the same size—$7^3/_4'' \times 5^3/_4''$. It is possible to increase or decrease the size of the card itself (that is, the border around the origami) to fit a specific envelope or other requirement, but the change should not be too extreme. Either of these adjustments are easily made, however keep the following cautions in mind:

- When enlarging the border, it is difficult to make the innermost folds if the border exceeds $10'' \times 7^1/_2''$.
- When reducing the border, be careful not to trim too much, or the structure may stick out when the card is folded in two.

Pop-up namecard.

Designing Your Own

Creating your own origami architecture is another way to put your design talents to work. It is a stimulating process, one that not only challenges your sense of design but your ability to deal with the abstract.

Constructing a miniature origami model is a step-by-step process, one in which the design must be drawn, tested, and refined several times over before a final usable plan is achieved. As each project has its own variables, what is offered here are general guidelines with ample illustration to illuminate the crea-'tive process.

It is important to possess some knowledge of drafting techniques. Moreover, although completing all the patterns in the book is not a prerequisite to making your own origami, you will need to fold at least ten or so projects before you are able to envision the relationship between the fold lines and resultant shapes.

1. Make a rough sketch. To this end gather as many visual reference materials as possible of the house you wish to make. A ground plan, a side view, a model of the house, and photographs of the real structure from every conceivable angle are all useful. After careful consideration of these materials (and whether the structure will be easy to represent as origami architecture), you can decide on the appearance of your structure: that is, which details to eliminate and which to emphasize.

2. Make an isometric drawing—in other words, a sketch of your planned structure in three dimensions. Remember that the structure must be made from just a single sheet of paper, so keep it simple in the beginning.

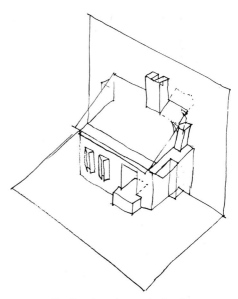

step 2 Sketch an isometric drawing.

3. Referring to the isometric drawing, map out the pattern on graph paper. (For this discussion the height is indicated by A and the depth by B.) If A equals B, the card will be symmetrical and the main mountain fold will be congruent with the central valley fold when flat. If, however, A and B are not equal, the mountain fold line will be parallel to, but not congruent with, the central crease. This may seem obvious, but is a point often overlooked. If you do not plan your structure accordingly, it will not fold to 90 degrees.

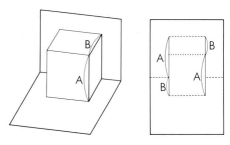

step 3 Calculate the height and depth.

4. Check the graph drawing. If it appears that some elements are a little too difficult to incorporate or that the measurements of the wall, the slope of the roof, or other aspects are not working, now is the time to alter them.

5. Trace your design onto suitable paper for trial construction. If there are any remaining awkward places, you will have to modify your plan. You may have to modify it any number of times before you have a structure that really works.

6. Check to see that none of the structure protrudes when the card is folded in half. Eliminate or further refine any troublesome elements.

To give you some perspective, both the front and top views are presented here along with the finished model.

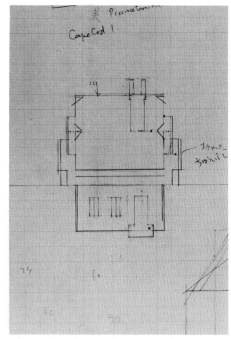

step 4   Transfer the design to graph paper.

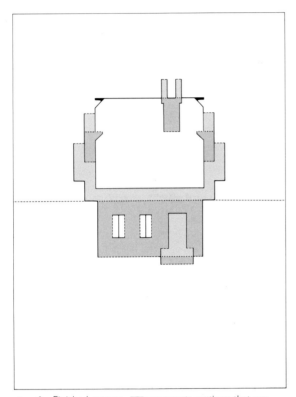

step 6   Finished pattern. ▨ represents sections that can seen from top; ▨ sections seen from front

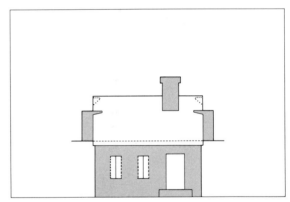

Sketch of finished house, front view.

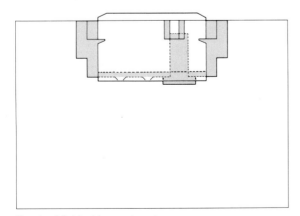

Sketch of finished house, top view.

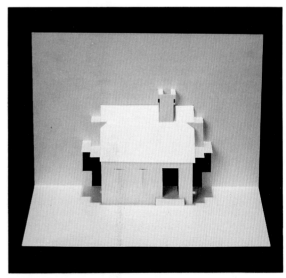

Finished house.

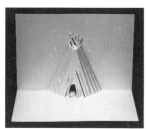

Level C

mountain fold ········ valley fold ──── cutting line ────

The tips of the support poles protruding at the top lend this origami structure its flavor, so cut them as neatly as possible. When you have finished cutting, press the center of the back side and the tepee will pop out.

Level C

········· mountain fold ———— valley fold ———— cutting line

In order to convey the rough-hewn, mud-daubed flavor of the house, cut the curved lines freehand. Cut out the ladder and clothes-drying platform on the right (made of logs in the original) in a similar fashion. The folds, however, should be as straight and as sharp as possible.

Level C

···· mountain fold   —— valley fold   —— cutting line

This work is explained in detail in Method 1, since it is the example house used. One additional note: Either during or after folding, insert the top edge of the roof into its slot. When the card is opened, the roof will slide out.

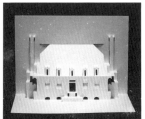

Level B

·····mountain fold ———valley fold ————cutting line

4

When you are ready to push out the form, press gently along the top of the front wall. At this stage the roof will be hanging in midair. When the folding is half done, press out the dormer windows carefully with a stylus or tweezers. Next, press out the chimneys, entrance, and staircase. Slowly work the roof down. Finish by gently pushing out the windows.

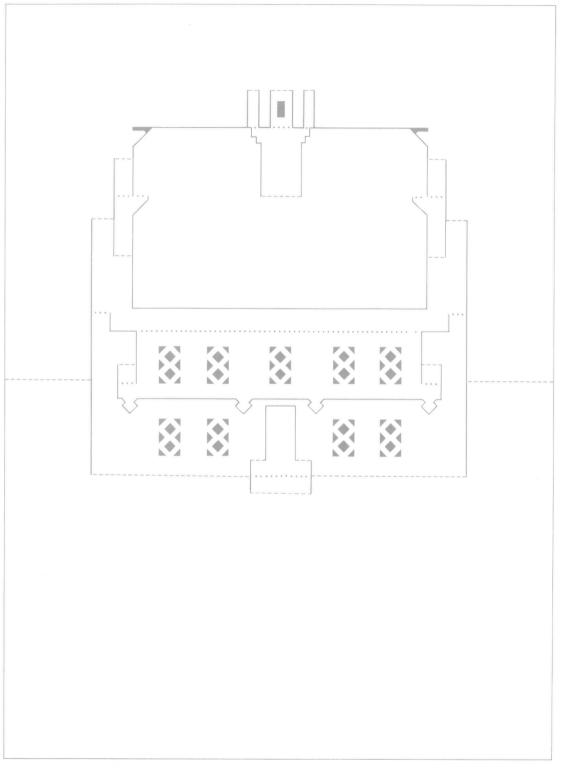

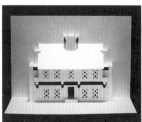

Level B

····· mountain fold ——— valley fold ——— cutting line

This house resembles number 3, with a protrusion at the second floor and a large chimney. The diamond pattern on the windows is very effective if you cut it out carefully. Cut the finely worked pendants slowly and accurately. The mountain folds of the second floor are hard to fold so a half-cut is strongly recommended.

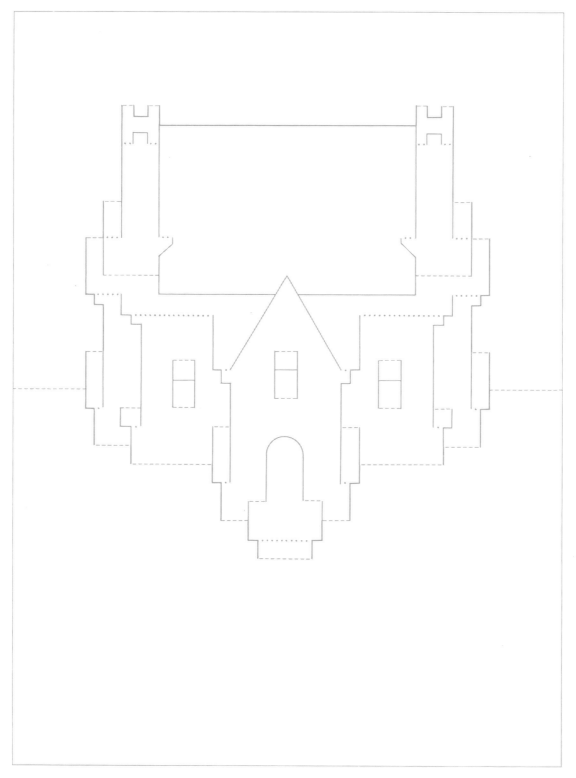

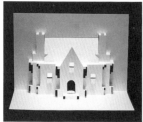

Level C

· · · · · mountain fold ——— valley fold ——— cutting line

The shape from the front is perfectly symmetrical, making the pushing-out step easier to visualize. First, gently press each side post, then press out the whole building. Take great care that your pressing does not result in unwanted folds. Never force the folding. If necessary, return the pattern to its flat state, check cutting and folding lines, and half-cut stubborn folds.

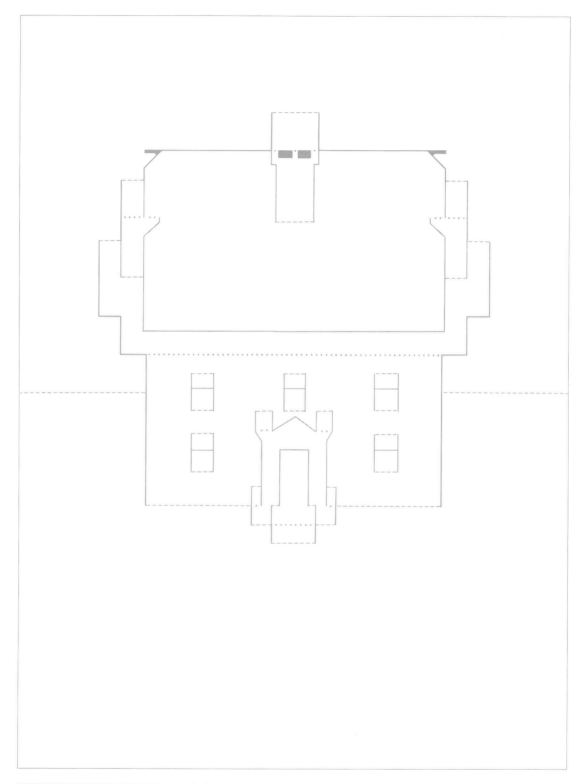

Level C

· · · · · mountain fold ——— valley fold ——— cutting line

The long mountain fold along the top of the second floor may be too stiff to fold, so half-cut it quite deeply. If the fold is not sharp, the bottom of the roof will not meet the ridge to hold it down.

Level C

· · · · · mountain fold ——— valley fold ——— cutting line

Despite being nonsymmetrical, this model is simple to make. Start by cutting the detailed areas—if you cut the major lines first, the paper will shift as you attempt to cut the detailed areas. When folding, on the other hand, you should always start from the major lines. Slowly press the entire structure out.

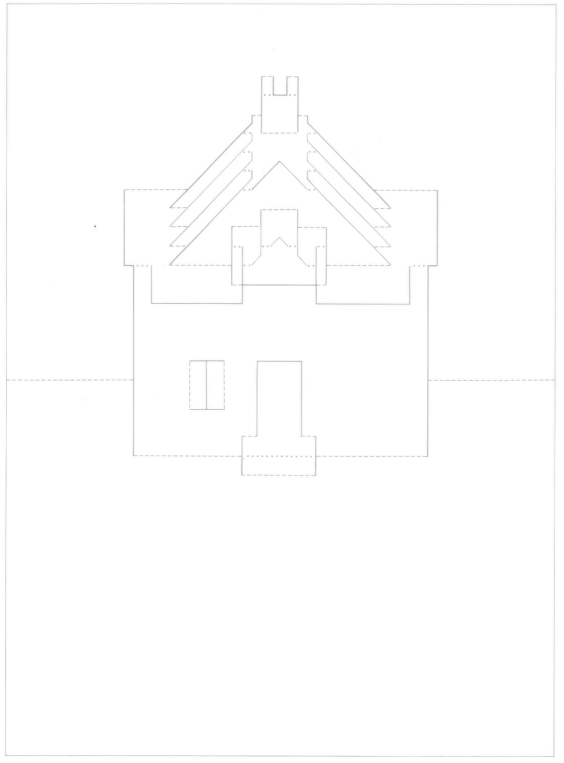

Level C

mountain fold   valley fold   cutting line

There is a number of methods by which to construct a gable in origami architecture. Here, the gable is represented by a series of parallel strips. In order for these origami gables to be effective the half-cuts at the base and top of each strip should be done with great precision, the series of three cut parallel.

Level B

mountain fold   valley fold   cutting line

Strongly half-cut the long mountain fold line above the colonnade. When you are ready to fold, begin with that same fold. Be very careful not to let any of the pillars bend as you push out the shape from the back.

Level B

· · · · mountain fold — — — valley fold ——— cutting line

After carefully folding the lines, cut the indicated lines, beginning with the detailed areas. From the back side of the roof, start folding the longest fold lines first, and, simultaneously if possible, push and pull with the tip of the stylus and the tweezers to neatly form the steps.

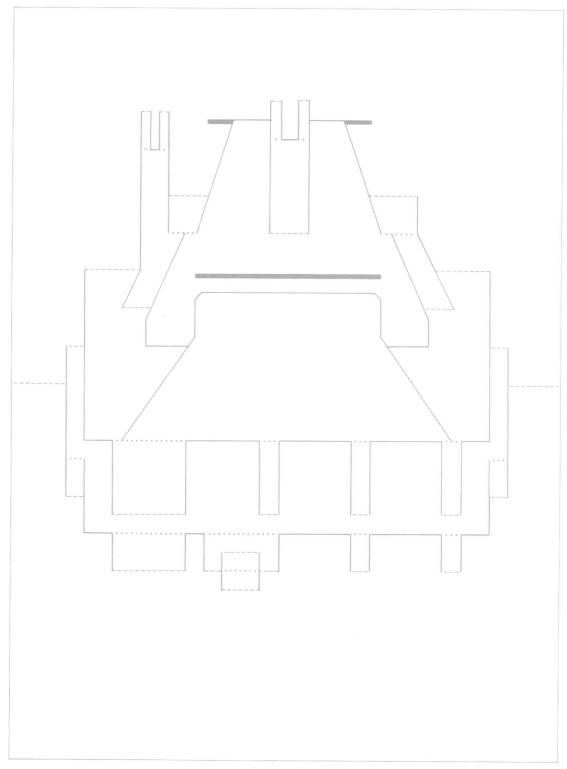

Level B   · · · · mountain fold   ——— valley fold   ——— cutting line

Because the roof consists of two slopes of different angles, the origami technique is rather special. Great care must be taken with the fold lines and the pillars. Cut, as usual, from the detailed areas.

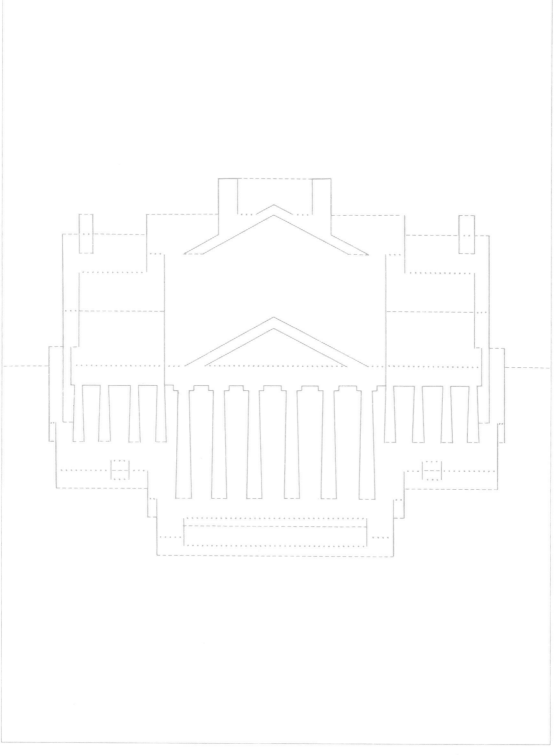

Level B   · · · · mountain fold   —— valley fold   —— cutting line

What brings this piece alive is the detail in the central columns. Not only should the capitals be clearly defined, but the columns should be cut in such a way as to give a "rounded," three-dimensional feeling to them and thus the whole central facade.

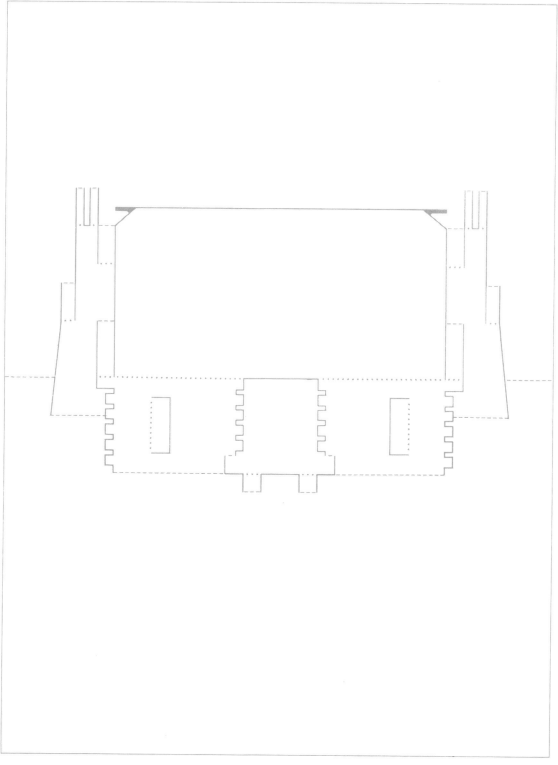

Level C

····· mountain fold ——— valley fold ——— cutting line

After folding the sloping roof, insert it into the slot. The special feature of this log cabin is the serrated effect of the wall, representing planks cut from cylindrical logs. The chimneys on either side should be pressed out firmly so that they stand as upright as possible.

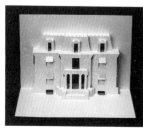

Level B

mountain fold · · · · · ·   valley fold ------   cutting line ------

Be sure to cut the curving sides of the mansard roof carefully. When pushing out the form, start with the mountain fold above the central second-story window and the ones separating the first and second levels. Next, from the area behind the dormer windows, push out the top valley fold with your fingertips, and then the dormer windows themselves. As you proceed, be careful not to bend the more fragile pillars and foundation.

Level A

· · · · · mountain fold ——— valley fold ——— cutting line

This is an example of a house constructed in the ornate Victorian style. The cutting is extremely complicated, so mistakes are likely. Even if you do make a mistake, it can be easily fixed (see Repairs). The finished product will be superb, in any event.

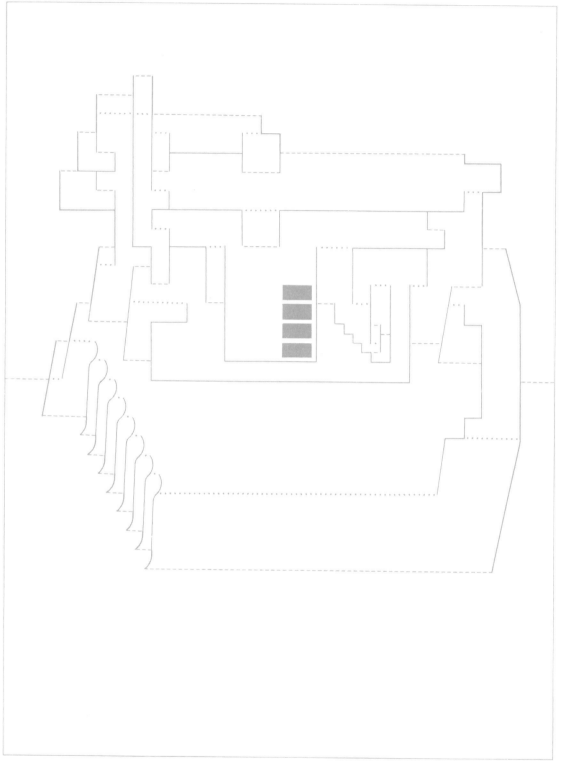

Level A

····· mountain fold   ──── valley fold   ──── cutting line

This house poses a fine test of your origami skills. It was designed to incorporate a modern, stepped waterfall (a pair of tweezers will come in useful for pulling out the waterfall's "ribs"). As a practical test of your origami craftsmanship, after successfully completing this pattern try making the waterfall "ribs" finer. If you can imagine the sound of water when you look at the card, you have truly realized the design.

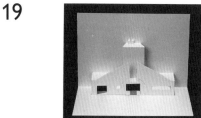

Level C

······· mountain fold   — — — valley fold   ———— cutting line

Your efforts should result in a triangular roof, split in the middle but linked by a strip of paper leading to the higher wall behind. The semicircular molding above the door is represented by cutting the paper. Use a proper circle cutter if you have one. The center of the circle should be on the entrance hall threshold line. When you are folding, remember to crease the convex line above the entrance very carefully before you fold the other lines.

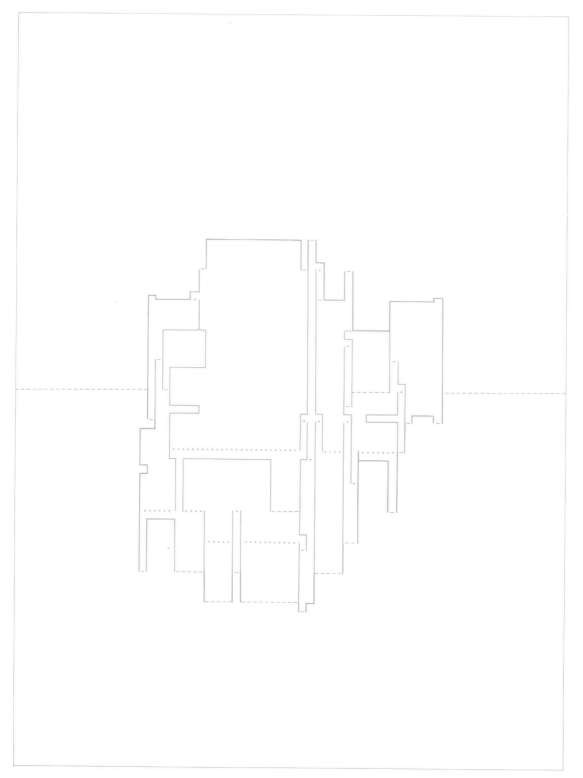

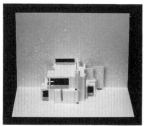

Level A+

·········· mountain fold ———— valley fold ———— cutting line

This last example is rated A+ because of the extremely detailed cutting necessary. Many of the cuts result in very thin strips, hence the fold lines are very short. If you are the slightest bit careless you may cut the paper, and, under the circumstances, repairs are not easy to make. Only attempt this model after carefully considering which are the mountain/valley fold lines and which the cutting lines. Again, you will find the tweezers of immense help.

Afterword

"Happy face" card.

When I meet people at my origami architecture exhibitions I am always asked how long I've been at it. In fact, I have only been designing origami architecture since 1981, but since all Japanese children are taught traditional origami from quite early on, I usually reply by giving my own age.

The next question is almost invariably, how long does it take to come up with a good idea? Well, I am a trained architect and my work involves planning, research, teaching, and so on. Though ideas occur quite suddenly—while I am engaged in my usual work—it is not quite that simple. If, however, I replied "about five minutes," the questioners—who are aware of the fact that I am occasionally paid for this activity—would be somewhat nonplussed. A more accurate answer would be five minutes to fifty years, and they are given a sense of the mystery of creation.

I had more than one motive when I started making origami architecture. At the time I was on the committee of the Japan Institute of Architects (JIA) where a particularly pressing issue was being debated.

In Japan, unlike Europe and America, the status of architecture as a profession (as opposed to, say, those of medicine and law) has yet to be firmly established. On the other hand, the image architecture has among young people today is fairly glamorous—an occupation blending art, fashion, and technology. The gap between image and hard reality is not appreciated among undergraduate architecture students, who receive a more thorough education in engineering than design.

To correct this imbalance became a goal of the JIA. Though we realized it was too late to do anything about trained architects, future generations could still be taught architectural aesthetics. The theory was that if such training starts very young—even in elementary school—a few will become excellent architects, while a majority of the rest ought to at least become discerning clients.

With this in mind, one afternoon I showed the other committee members an example of origami architecture that had been conceived and created some time before the conference. It was a booklet made up of a number of cards cut, tied, folded, and affixed to an accordion-folded pasteboard base. As each section was unfolded a three-dimensional shape emerged and took shape, seeming to bloom before one's eyes.

I opened the sections one by one and each drew a more resounding response

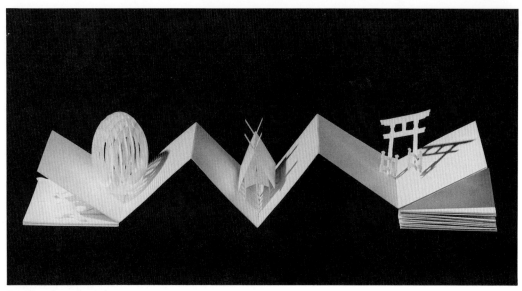

Booklet of pop-ups.

than the last. Everyone was impressed. They all agreed that if a book were produced around the concept of origami architecture, not only could anyone enjoy making the origami but it would be a much more effective way of training future architects than any lectures on the subject. Origami might, then, encourage students to conceive and plan imaginative, original buildings while at the same time instilling in them a higher sense of architectural aesthetics.

Unaccustomed to such flattering acceptance and quite carried away by it all, I began to make cards in earnest. Apart from the series above, which opened to 180 degress, I constructed patterns which unfolded to a full 360 degrees and others which, by cutting strips of paper and laying them on a flat card in an overlapping fashion, created the illusion of a three-dimensional structure.

I wasn't always so preoccupied. It all started with a much simpler card some years ago. New Year's had rolled around again and it was time to send the traditional year-end greeting cards. Previously, I had always sent cards based on cheerful sketches I coerced my children into making for me, and these were always well received. My children, however, were growing up and had started talking about making their own cards. I couldn't continue with that particular tactic, and, unwilling to send store-bought cards, I was at a loss as to what to do.

I decided on a 90-degree "happy face" card that year. I made five hundred cards—each by hand. When my friends responded enthusiastically I realized what a good idea it had been. In 1982, acting on the advice of my teacher, Kiyoshi Seike, I first displayed a collection of cards at the Ginza Matsuya's design gallery.

That exhibition was the beginning. Since then, my work has been displayed in exhibitions not only in Japan but in America, Denmark, Holland, Switzerland, Italy, and elsewhere. Now, in America and Europe, students, teachers and other enthusiasts hold origami architecture exhibitions of their own. All this activity is quite gratifying and stimulating. For, indeed, the possibilities are endless: from the miniature pop-up namecard (in Variations, page 38) to the formal printed invitation here. I cannot but hope that more and more of you will rise to the challenge of creating your own works.

To create the designs in this book, I had to delve deeply into the history of traditional American houses. I researched many more structures than I ultimately included. While thus engaged, an interesting trend emerged. It became apparent that many of the preserved structures were at one time or another forgotten, their value overlooked. At the time when each was to be demolished

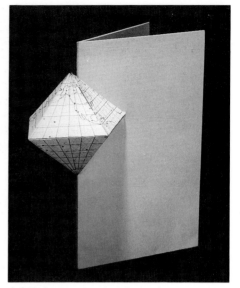

Layered card.   A 360-degree origami card.

it was only the voices of a farsighted few, or in many cases a single person, who saved these wonderful structures. Moreover, voluntary organizations were often formed for the preservation and restoration of these buildings. They were mostly successful, and we are all indebted to those people. Not only in America but all over the world identical situations have arisen, and it is only the clear-sighted few who speak up.

To realize of the value of the land, its history, its monuments large and small, is to realize one's own value and understand one's place—a truth most of us come to know in time. The origami architecture here is one of the many ways in which to nurture an appreciation of America's architecture and its legacy, and in a broader, more universal sense to understand architecture and its role in making the world truly suitable for human life.

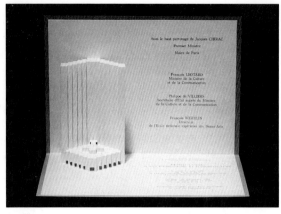

Formal invitation card.

Bibliography

Foley, Mary Mix. *The American House.* Tokyo: Kajima Institute Publishing Co., Japanese ed., 1981.

Seike Kiyoshi, Yagi Koji, and Wada Hisashi. *American House.* Tokyo: Nenkin Jutaku Fukushi Kyokai, 1986. Tokyo: Kodansha, Japanese ed., 1987.

Smith, G. E. Kidder. *The Architecture of the United States,* vols. 1–3. New York: Anchor Books, Anchor Press/Doubleday, 1981.

Walker, Lester. *American Shelter.* New York: Overlook Press, 1981.

Acknowledgments

Many people have lent their assistance directly and indirectly in the making of this book. Though it is not possible to credit all of the people who so generously helped, I would like to take this opportunity to thank the following few.

I am deeply indepted to Professor Koji Yagi for his invaluable guidance regarding American architectural history, to Toshiaki Nakazawa for his impeccable research and line drawings, and to Keiko Nakazawa for the picture-perfect origami that appears on the jacket.

Well-deserved thanks must also go to the members of my design lab, whose diligence never flagged. They include Naomi Ando, Keiko and Hitoshi Nakamura, Akiko Nakano, Ryuzo Ohno, Yoko Sasaki, Nobuhiro Yamahata, and Katsuhiko Yashiro.

For the opportunity to represent their structures, I offer my thanks to Robert Venturi, Peter Eisenman, and Kenzo Tange.

A book such as this requires, indeed often depends on, the generosity and good will of many unsung heroes. My deep gratitude to the many individuals, organizations, and institutions who patiently answered my numerous queries about the houses in this book. Though I cannot list them all here, I hope they receive some satisfaction from the treatment the houses they work so carefully to preserve have been given here.

For their support over the years, my deep-felt thanks also goes to Shozo Baba, Takeshi Ishido, Toshio Nakamura, Masato Nakatani, Yoshio Yoshida of The Japan Architect Co., Aiko Hasegawa of Kajima Inc., and Kazukiyo Matsuba and Itsuo Sakane of the Asahi Shimbun.

For their enthusiasm and continuous encouragement, I am obligated to sculptor Takamichi Ito; Kiyoshi Seike, professor emeritus; Yoshiko Ebihara of Gallery 91 in New York; and Seinosuke Kimura, Teiichi Takahashi, Tsutomu Ushiyama, and Ryosuke Yoshioka of the Japan Institute of Architects.

Last but certainly not forgotten, I wish to acknowledge my editors, Katsuhiko Sakiyama, Michiko Uchiyama, and Barry Lancet, for their dedication and energetic efforts in bringing this volume to life.

定価1,800円
in Japan